MAKING MAPS
Where's the Party?

Based on the Math Monsters™ public television series, developed in cooperation with the National Council of Teachers of Mathematics (NCTM).

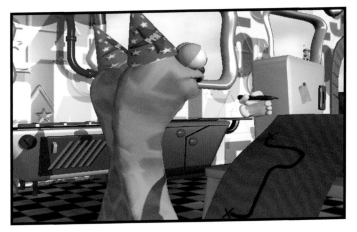

by John Burstein

Reading consultant: Susan Nations, M.Ed., author/literacy coach/consultant
Math curriculum consultants: Marti Wolfe, M.Ed., teacher/presenter; Kristi Hardi-Gilson, B.A., teacher/presenter

WEEKLY (WR) READER®
EARLY LEARNING LIBRARY

Please visit our web site at: **www.earlyliteracy.cc**
For a free color catalog describing Weekly Reader® Early Learning Library's list
of high-quality books, call 1-877-445-5824 (USA) or 1-800-387-3178 (Canada).
Weekly Reader® Early Learning Library's fax: (414) 336-0164.

Library of Congress Cataloging-in-Publication Data

Burstein, John.
    Making maps: where's the party? / by John Burstein.
       p. cm. — (Math monsters)
    Summary: The four math monsters figure out how to draw a map when someone
they have invited to a party does not know how to reach their castle.
    ISBN 0-8368-3811-4 (lib. bdg.)
    ISBN 0-8368-3826-2 (softcover)
    1. Map drawing—Juvenile literature. [1. Map drawing.] I. Title.
GA130.B87   2003
526—dc21
                                                    2003045049

This edition first published in 2004 by
Weekly Reader® Early Learning Library
330 West Olive Street, Suite 100
Milwaukee, WI 53212 USA

Original Math Monsters™ animation: Destiny Images
Art direction, cover design, and page layout: Tammy Gruenewald
Editor: JoAnn Early Macken

Printed in the United States of America

1 2 3 4 5 6 7 8 9 07 06 05 04 03

You can enrich your children's mathematical experience by working
with them as they tackle the Corner Questions in this book. Create
a special notebook for recording their mathematical ideas.

Mapping and Math

Mapping can help children begin to organize and master the world
around them. It will help them develop their spatial sense
in regard to direction, distance, and location.

Meet the Math Monsters™

Addison thinks
math is fun.
"I solve problems
one by one."

ADDISON

Mina flies
from here to there.
"I look for answers
everywhere."

MINA

Multiplex
sure loves to laugh.
"Both my heads
have fun with math."

MULTIPLEX

Split is friendly
as can be.
"If you need help,
then count on me."

SPLIT

We're glad you want to take a look
at the story in our book.

We know that as you read, you'll see
just how helpful math can be.

Let's get started. Jump right in!
Turn the page, and let's begin!

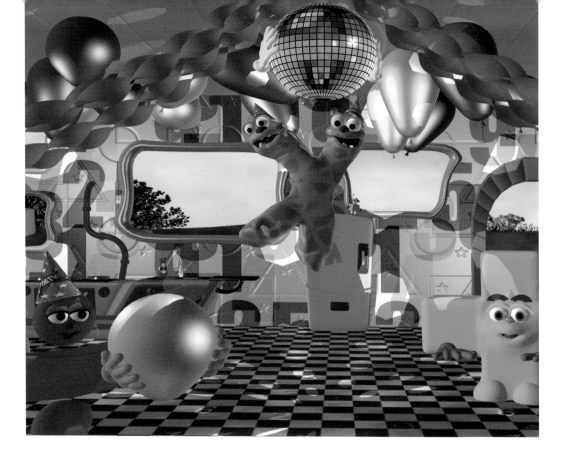

The Math Monsters were planning a party.
They wanted all their friends to come.

They wrote cards to everyone.
The cards said,
"We will eat cake
and blow up balloons.
We will play games
and sing happy tunes."

What kind of parties do you like to go to?

Multiplex put all the cards in a bag. He put the
bag in the mailbox.

"There are so many cards," he said.

The next day, Big Bill called the
Math Monsters.

"Hello," he said. "I got your card.
I want to come to your party, but I
do not know how to get to your
castle. Can you help me?"

How can the monsters help Big Bill?

"We will send you a map," said Addison.
"I will draw it," said Multiplex.

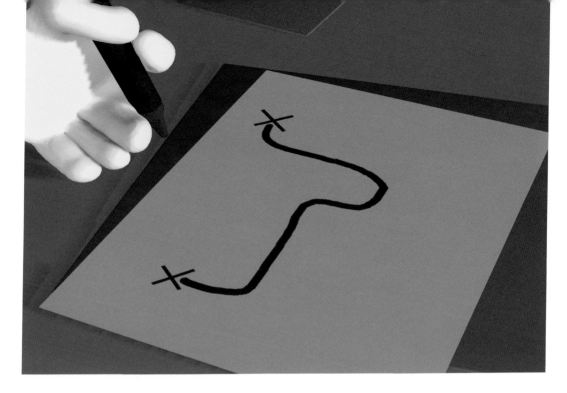

Multiplex took some paper. He drew a long line. He made two marks.

"The mark on top is for our castle, where Big Bill needs to go. The mark on the bottom is where Big Bill is now," he said.

"That is a nice map," said Mina. She mailed it to Big Bill.

Do you think this map will help Big Bill find his way to the castle?

9

Big Bill got the map. He looked and looked at it.

"This is just a line," he said. "It will not help me find my way."

He called the Math Monsters again.

"Hello," said Multiplex.

"Hello," said Big Bill. "I need some more help. Can you draw some landmarks on your map?"

"Landmarks?" asked Multiplex. "What are landmarks?"

What do you think a landmark is?

"Landmarks are special
things I will see on my way
to the castle," said Big Bill.
"You can pick things that
are big and colorful, like

the Monster Town Flagpole,

the water tower,

the big statue,

or the diner."

"If you draw them on the map, they will help me find my way to your castle."

How can landmarks on the map help Big Bill find his way?

13

"I will draw some landmarks right now," said Multiplex. "They are sure to help."

"I am not sure where the landmarks go on the map," said Multiplex. "I will draw them where they look nice."

He sent the new map with the landmarks to Big Bill.

Do you think this map will help Big Bill?

15

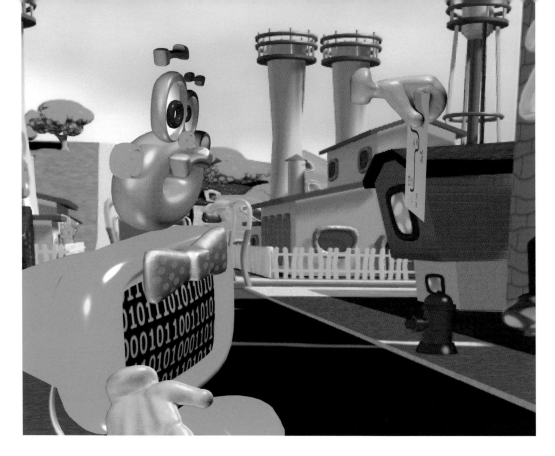

Big Bill got the map. He went out to try it.

"Oh no," he said. "This cannot help me at all."

He went back inside and called the Math Monsters.

"Multiplex, you did not put the landmarks in the right places," he said.

"I will try to fix it," said Multiplex.

Multiplex hung up the phone. He said, "I want to help Big Bill, but I do not know where to put the landmarks."

"I know how we can find out," said Mina.

How can Mina find out where to put the landmarks?

17

"Let's go into town. We will see where the landmarks really are," said Mina. "Then we can make a new map that is sure to help."

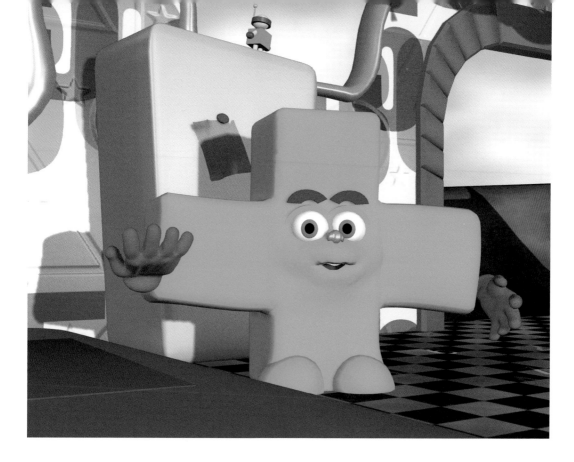

"Is there anything else we can put on the map to make it better?" asked Addison.

What other things might help the Math Monsters make a good map?

"We can draw the streets and write their names," said Mina.

The monsters looked at the street signs.

Multiplex drew the streets on
the map. He wrote their names.
He drew the landmarks where
they belonged.

*What do you think
the new map
will look like?
Will it be better?*

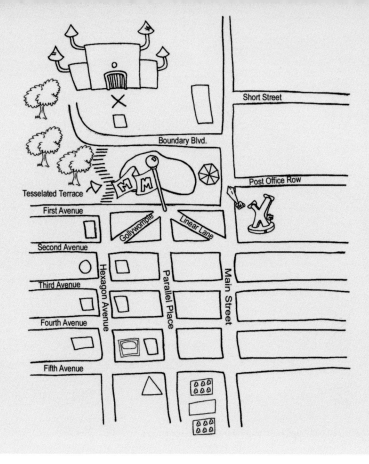

"This map looks great!" said Addison.
"It will work much better," said Split.
"Let's send it to Big Bill," said Mina.

Big Bill was very happy with the new map. "I love parties," he said. He sang a little song.

"I am going to a party.
I am going right away.
I am going to a party.
The map shows me the way."

Can you draw a map of your neighborhood? Can you think of any other kinds of helpful maps?

ACTIVITIES

Page 5 Ask children to talk about their favorite kinds of parties. Discuss what goes into planning and preparing for a party.

Page 7 Find a map at home or school, such as a world map, road map, or atlas. Talk about an imaginary trip you want to take and discuss with the children how the map can help you find your way.

Page 9 Help the children notice that a single line drawn on a blank piece of paper does not provide much directional information.

Pages 11, 13 Ask children to close their eyes and imagine they are walking home from the playground. Ask them to think of natural or man-made objects they see along the way, such as a post office, a swing set, a statue, or a big tree. These are landmarks.

Pages 15, 17 Make two maps of your classroom or kitchen. Include the same objects in both maps, but make only one map reflect the correct placement of the objects. Have children compare the maps. Explain why landmarks must be placed accurately to be helpful.

Pages 19, 21 With the children, make a map of your neighborhood. In addition to landmarks, talk about what else might go on the map to help people find their way, such as streets, parks, buildings, and signs.

Page 23 Have fun discovering the many ways people represent the world and the universe using maps, such as maps of the ocean floor, maps of the moon, and maps of space.